Dear

You have known me
all along —

Sheila Kennedy

Sheila Kennedy

You Had It All Along

5 Keys to Unlocking the POWER of Confidence at your Core

You Had It All Along
5 Keys to Unlocking the Power of Confidence
At Your Core
©2013 by Sheila Kennedy

Expert Insights Publishing
1001 East WT Harris Blvd #247
Charlotte, NC 28213

ISBN: 978-0-9837379-7-1

Author: Sheila Kennedy
Cover Design: Robert Miller
Photography: Clear Digital Photography
Design: Terry Z
Edited by: Pam Murphy

15 14 13 12 11   1 2 3 4 5

—Dedication—

This book is dedicated to my beautiful daughter, Shannon.
If it weren't for you, I may still be living a "good enough" life
and hiding behind my game face.
You inspired me to find the courage to build a better life
and to write this blueprint for women
who settle for less than they deserve.
Thank you, Shannon, for your patience and love.
I pray these words show you how to live a more brilliant life
—that is definitely what you are made for!
Don't ever settle, my child, you deserve God's best!

—Acknowledgements—

God—Thank you for every second that led to this moment. This book is about qualifying the called vs. calling the qualified. I am humbled by Your trust in me.

Mom and Rev—Your support has been unwavering. You have my eternal gratitude.

Karen Ryan—The hours you spent editing the book and supporting me—I couldn't have done it without you.

Susan Rider—J29 Project was born from your compassion. I will forever be grateful for that email!

Jenohn LeShea Smith, Linda Lindsey, Marsha Booth, Sarah Hart and Ginny Whitt—When the days were really hard, you held me up!

Jennifer Rapke—You helped me get my life back! Thank you!

Sarah Newton—P.O.W.E.R. exists because of your support.

The Ladies of Mastermind B—Therese, Mary Lyn, Joy and Jamie—Thank you for the chiseling, encouragement and love!

The Launching Ladies—Cynthia, Joanne and Karen—Your support has been a bright spot through the whole process!

Rich Bradley, John Flynn and Tom Kennedy—I can't imagine how I would have gotten here without your help!

Robert Miller—You nailed it! You have a brilliant career ahead! It has been an honor to work with you.

Lou Allen of Clear Digital Photography, Kristen Cartagena, John Bumpus, and Shannon O.—Thank you for your artistry!

Viki Winterton and the Ladies of *Wounded? Survive! Thrive!!!* —Your courage and example inspire me! It is an honor to be in your company!

—Table of Contents—

—Introduction—

Are you Feeling Confident?

Many women would say yes, but in reality they hide behind a mask of false confidence. They cover their insecurities to make it look like they have it all together on the outside but the inside story is much different. They stay stuck in a sea of mediocrity because they are secure in the safety of what they know and repel opportunities to live and succeed outside of their comfort zone.

They also tend to struggle with:
   * Making the income they deserve.
   * Unsatisfying relationships at home and at work.
   * Being paralyzed by indecision.
   * The tug at their heart to pursue their passion.

Sound familiar? It might be your story, but it doesn't have to stay your story. You possess the POWER to remove the mask and live confidently. It is time to pursue your passion, make the income you deserve and engage in relationships that fulfill you.

You Had It All Along is the catalyst you have been waiting for to finally release the powerful confidence found deep in your core.

Sheila Kennedy outlines five keys vital to unlocking an unshakable faith in yourself that will launch you into a life filled with contentment, meaning and success.

—Chapter One—
The Search

Have you ever had the experience when you are searching for something and the very thing that you are looking for is right in front of you? Imagine the busy woman who is on the phone and says to the person on the other line, "If I could just find my phone, we can schedule that meeting" or searching for your glasses when they are resting comfortably on top of your head. Sometimes the very thing that we are searching for has been there all along.

Confidence can be like that. We were born with it but we can't always find it. We enter this world wrapped in a blanket of confidence, but that rarely lasts for long. Somehow the world has a tendency of tearing away at that blanket until it is tattered and torn. Eventually we forget about the warmth of true confidence and tolerate the cold without it.

Like the Wizard of Oz, we end up hiding behind the curtain of false confidence, so our imperfections and weaknesses are hidden from the world. From the outside, it looks like we are mighty and power-ful, but the truth is we are too scared to reveal who we completely are. Too many hits from the world telling you who or what you are **not** compel you to bury your confidence to depths you cannot con-sciously fathom. Your faith in who you are may end up buried so deeply that it seems impossible to draw upon it when needed.

It is my sincere hope that the words on these pages help you to begin releasing the confidence that you have possessed all along. "Fake it 'til you make it" should not be your mantra. You were created for more than that.

As I struggled through my own discovery process, I determined that there are five keys to unlocking the power that confidence at your core brings. As the five keys are detailed, get involved as deeply as you can. The more honest you are, the more heartfelt your confidence will be. You deserve that faith in yourself. You deserve all of the benefits that come with confidence at your core.

What Areas of your Life would Benefit from Unlocking Confidence at your Core?

—Chapter Two—
The Game Face

What you say is not always the same as what you believe. I remember a time in my life when I would have publicly scoffed at the idea that I lacked confidence. I behaved in a way that exuded it. Walking into rooms like I was the boss, I succeeded at things that I probably shouldn't have been able to. The various facets of my life looked really good from the external looking glass.

All the while, I was feeling anything but confident. I literally was dying inside. I became a perfectionist because I constantly felt imperfect. I felt that I needed to measure up and prove my worth, seeking external affirmation because I did not feel it inside. Constantly driving to do more and be more because I felt like LESS all of the time.

I became really good at hiding how I felt. Authenticity was a dirty word for me and admitting that I didn't have it all together was not going to happen. I was so afraid that my shortcomings and fears would be revealed, I went to great lengths to keep them hidden.

I learned to put on my game face. If you are reading this book, you may be familiar with it. On the outside, you make everything look good enough. You perform decently at your job, your relationships appear fine, you experience a moderate level of success, you smile and all seems right and well in your world externally. What is happening on the inside is another story. You feel frustrated, fearful, tired and wanting more.

I believe that we are conditioned at an early age not to show how we truly feel. We especially do not want to claim our imperfections. They make us appear weak and we would never want to give someone else an unfair advantage over us. We hide all of those things that would make others question our value and our worth. We employ tactics to cover our weaknesses like we apply concealer to the bags under our eyes. *As if it could be that easy!*

You can cover up your insecurity all you want, but eventually it surfaces. What you can't hide, you then try to ignore. Like those moments at the end of the day when you take that concealer off and you see your raw, unpolished self. Rather than look at yourself in the mirror, it is easier to go to bed then to see what you really look like.

The duality of the game face zaps your energy. The act of hiding takes a great deal of effort. The idea of addressing why you have bags under your eyes is much more time consuming and exhausting than just slapping on the concealer every morning. You wind up stuck in a holding pattern of survival because the very idea of anything more is too overwhelming. You endure wearing the mask in your life, because the thought of taking it off would leave you too vulnerable.

I first wore my game face when I was about seven years old and no bigger than a minute. I was playing softball and the baseball bat was taller than I was.

19

Every time I was at bat, I was walked, never actually hitting the ball. Towards the end of the season, I finally hit the ball and it dribbled to the pitcher. As soon as the ball connected with the bat, I started to cry. Running to first base with tears in my eyes, I was easily thrown out.

My dad came running over to me and yanked me off to the side, yelling at me that I was never to cry when I got thrown out. He ranted about showing poor sportsmanship. I remember looking up at him through my tear-filled eyes and said, "Daddy, I am not crying because I got out. I am crying because I was so happy I finally hit the ball." He reminded me that there was no crying on the ball field no matter what the reason was.

That stayed with me – I did not want to let him down. A few years later he passed away. As a dramatic ten year old with a tear in my eye, I remember saying to my mother on the day of his funeral, "It wasn't every day that you have to bury your dad." Her response to me was that there was a time and a place to act like that and today wasn't it. She was trying so hard to keep her emotions under control and I understand that now, but then and for a very long time after that, I thought the message was — don't show how you really feel.

Later when I was about to be married to an Army Officer, as an engagement gift, my fiancé gave me manuals on "How to be an Army Wife." I got the message that appearance was everything and no matter what was happening, I was expected to support him with a smile on my face. My task was to make everything look just fine. As archaic as that sentiment seems, it was reiterated many times over during the course of his Army career.

Years later when life was definitely not fine and dysfunction transformed into an abusive situation, I still smiled. The Army was no longer a part of our lives and I was trying to build a business. Instead of building his career, I was trying to build my own. I remember thinking who would want to do business with me if they knew how messed up my life was? I became extremely good at putting on the game face every day.

Take a minute or two to recall the events that happened in your life that may have triggered the act of putting on your game face. What events took place that may have caused you to think you couldn't be authentic?

If you have ever worn the game face, it is time to remove it once and for all. Living that dual life hoping that no one yanks off your mask is exhausting and fruitless. You deserve to have yourself wrapped in that blanket of confidence again.

You have weaknesses, but you also have strengths. You experience fear, but you also experience faith. You have difficulties and trials in life, but you also have periods of ease and prosperity. It is that duality that delivers confidence.

You are an amazing combination of all things — things that should initiate a celebration.

It isn't enough for me to tell you, you must experience it and discover it for yourself.

Let the adventure begin ...

Is there a defining moment that caused you to question true and authentic confidence?

—Chapter Three—
The Moment of Recognition

You may cruise along in game face mode until something forces you to examine the price you pay for burying your worth.

The moment of crisis occurs when you feel compelled not to show who you really are, but do not possess the energy to hide anymore. You acknowledge that you want to be real, but you are held hostage by the fear of rejection if you are honest. There is constant worry that you may be found out and declared a fraud.

That moment of crisis knocks on your door because there is a disconnect between trying to juggle both the fear of being exposed and the safety of hiding. There usually isn't enough energy to deal with both.

It is in these moments that you realize how much you have cheated yourself. You realize that the cost of not living confidently has been huge. There are some very tangible benefits that come with feeling confidence at your core and you shouldn't miss out on those one moment longer than you already have.

Recognize that you have had a choice all along and it is time now to choose differently.

Have you had a moment of recognition? What was it?

Chapter Four

The Cost of Burying Confidence

The stakes are high. Life changes dramatically when you live without the mask of false confidence. Before you can embrace the difference, I think it is vital to outline the cost of living with less than confidence at your core.

—You think less of yourself and place more value on the opinions of others. You believe less in your abilities and focus more on your faults.

—You lack the energy and the health to make positive changes, so you coast on what you have always done and get stuck in a sea of mediocrity.

—Your income stands still or your financial success feels hampered. You tend to make lateral moves rather than climbing up the ladder of success.

—You rely on validation from outside sources because you cannot find it from within. You spend your time performing for compliments, and every negative comment, awkward glance, and disengagement holds you hostage and freezes forward motion.

—You get stuck in a negative cycle of fear, self-doubt and insecurity that spins so fast you can't see your own worth.

—You have a difficult time making decisions. You miss deadlines, flip flop, and are easily influenced by what other people want you to do. You fail to trust your own decision-making capabilities.

—You put everyone else's needs before your own.

—You justify why you don't engage in self-care.

—You struggle in your relationships with others. There is not a balance and you don't feel acknowledged.

—You allow new adventures or opportunities to pass you by. You cling to the safety net of what you know rather than attempting to reach new heights.

Those are some pretty high costs, if you ask me. The good news is that it doesn't have to be that way. You can turn it around right now, this very day. You have had the solution all along buried underneath the mask. It is time give yourself the gift of confidence felt deep at your core.

What are YOUR costs for burying your confidence?

What is it

—Chapter Five—
Confidence at Your Core

Confidence at Your Core is an unshakable faith in your abilities. It is knowing that you have everything you need to come out on top at the end of the day – no matter what kind of day it has been. It is understanding that you may not personally possess all of the skills you need to overcome every situation, but believing that you will know how to find what you may lack.

This confidence is a foundational belief that everything happens for a purpose and points you in the direction of something better. Even those events that feel harmful and throw you for a loop are not designed to hurt you, but to strengthen you. Knowing that the universe has not conspired to condemn you to a lifetime of hardship, but provides you opportunities to learn and to grow makes everything a bit more "survivable."

Don't confuse confidence at your core with the eternal absence of self-doubt or fear. Those moments may still occur *occasionally*, but there is a distinct difference when you do. When you do experience those feelings, they are a temporary, often momentary, feeling. You see what is causing them and can put into perspective whatever the trigger is. That is achievable because you truly believe that you are capable and you push through it rather than be defined by it. You know that your ability is bigger than your fear and insecurity!

For me, my journey to believe in myself has been a long and arduous one. That blanket of confidence that I crashed into the world wearing became threadbare. It was in a moment of feeling completely hopeless, that the truth was revealed.

I certainly struggled after my divorce. I was a single mom and held a steady job that I didn't want so the bills could get paid. I also owned a business that fed my passion, but not my mouth. Feeling completely broken, I had left an abusive marriage in hopes that I could redeem some semblance of self-worth.

Most days I was too tired to even think about my self-worth — let alone DO something to improve it. Bogged down in shame, guilt and negativity, I questioned a million times why I ever thought I deserved anything better.

A friend watching me struggle sent me the Bible passage, Jeremiah 29:11. "For I know the plans I have for you," declared the Lord. "Plans to prosper you and not to harm you. Plans to give you hope and a future." Reading those words became a pivotal point for me.

I realized two things when I read that passage. One was that I was worth it! If God had a plan for me, then I must be worthy of it. No one would waste their time or resources on someone who wasn't. I desperately needed to be reminded of that.

The second thing I realized was that I was going to experience bad things, but they were to prepare me for something better. I didn't have to know what "better" was, but I needed to believe that every heartache, disappointment and broken moment was strengthening me so I could discover it. When I accepted those two ideas, my outlook on life began to improve dramatically.

The transformation began with that moment of enlightenment that in return sparked an intense time of introspection. I realized that the hardships were opportunities to use the gifts and talents I had been given. There were choices I had made that did not honor the gift that I am to this world. I decided I would no longer play the victim card. I could choose to play a different hand.

Mediocrity and mere survival were not what I was gifted with — I had been given everything I needed to live a fulfilling and meaningful life. The obstacles I encounter are a vehicle to remind me of my fortitude. I am now confident that I can thrive in spite of what was standing in my way. The hardest realization of all, was understanding that the biggest obstacle holding me back was ME.

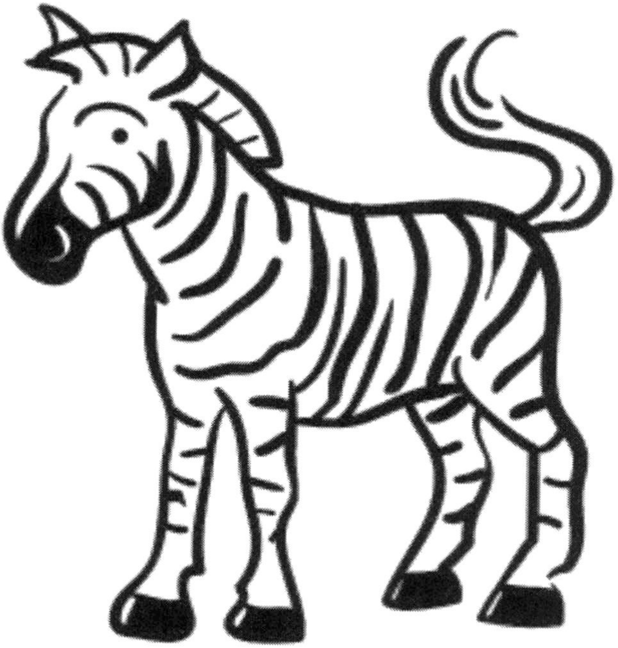

—Chapter Six—

The Power of the Zebra

Traveling through self-inspection, I realized that I possessed a power that I didn't acknowledge I had. The ability to choose is the most empowering gift ever. I don't necessarily get to choose myself out of a situation, but I do get to choose my reaction. Rarely do I speak in absolutes, but this is one of those times. I can always choose how I react to whatever is going on in my life. There were some hard times when I remember uttering the words, "I don't have a choice." That's crap – I did then and I do now. So do you!

What in the world does a zebra have to do with any of this? The zebra print is a visual cue that reminds me I have the power to choose. I read a poem written by Shel Silverstein who asked the zebra if it was black with white stripes or white with black stripes. The zebra answered with several questions such as "Was he noisy in a quiet world or quiet in a noisy world." Seeing the zebra print helps me remember that I have the power to choose.

So today and every day from here on out, please remember that you too have the POWER to choose.

The black and white of the zebra also reminds me of the duality that I faced each day as described in the previous chapter. Life is about balance. There are positive and negative traits in my character but it is the combination of both of those things that creates something truly amazing. It is in embracing all of me that leaves me feeling truly confident and whole.

Let's celebrate for a moment the choice you have made by reading this book. You have decided to at least explore the option of discovering a new way of thinking about yourself. That is a huge step! It took me what seemed like forever to get to that point and my only wish is that I had started it sooner.

Congratulations for coming this far – for deciding that you are worth it and for understanding that a change needs to be made in order to move forward.

Let's have a parade just for you! You can sit on top of a zebra, leading a legion of fans cheering your success, and celebrating that you are making the choice to unlock the confidence waiting at your core.

You are so worth it!

—Chapter Seven—
Let's Celebrate!

One idea that comes to mind as you begin this path to empowerment is that you should celebrate each step along the way. You will not continue to do anything if it doesn't ultimately make you feel good. It is vital to discover ways that you can celebrate the positive choices you make.

Celebrations do not have to be big and they don't have to cost anything. They can be as simple as taking a walk outside to enjoy nature. Your list of ways to celebrate is an opportunity to get in touch with what motives you to keep going. Money could be thrown on your lap, but if money isn't a motivator for you, then you won't continue to do this work. It is important to tap into what motivates your soul to make changes.

Celebrations can take many forms and most of the ideas you may think of will be externally motivated. Do not dismiss the internal practice of relishing the moment. When you have done something celebration worthy – give yourself at least a moment or two to recognize the accomplishment and how you feel.

In other words, if you are at work and you take a stand for yourself, take a moment to reflect on what you just accomplished. By all means choose an external celebration too, but you may find that once you tap into how good accomplishment feels that will become your major motivation to continue.

Take the time to write down a list of external rewards that would motivate you to continued action.
What would extend your feeling of accomplishment?

Here are a few suggestions to help you get started ...

⇒ Take a bath

⇒ Go for a walk

⇒ Enjoy a treat to eat or drink

⇒ Read a book or magazine

⇒ Take a nap

⇒ Dream about the future for ten minutes

⇒ Create a piece of art

⇒ Spend time working on a hobby

⇒ Watch a movie

⇒ Make a meal to enjoy

⇒ Color in a coloring book

⇒ Read or write a poem

⇒ Contact someone who makes you smile

⇒ Feed the ducks

⇒ Laugh

⇒ Pray

⇒ Polish your nails

⇒ Smell the flowers

⇒ Volunteer

—Let's Celebrate, 7

How will you celebrate?

—Chapter Eight—
Unlocking the P.O.W.E.R.

The five keys to unlocking confidence at your core can be wrapped up in one short acronym and that is **P.O.W.E.R.** This is where the rubber meets the road. These are the steps to take to climb out of the holding pattern of the status quo and claim what has been buried inside of you all along. Commit to doing the work so that you can enjoy all of the benefits.

Let's examine both sides of the confidence coin. Having been on both, I can tell you that I enjoy the confident side much better. Hopeless, torn, exhausted and hidden are no way to live. I can honestly say that those feelings have fallen away and have been replaced with hope, clarity, energy and authenticity which ultimately equates to more success!

When you travel through the five keys of **P.O.W.E.R.**, you discover that you have value. You see that you matter and when you matter ...

—You respect yourself. When you display self-respect other people will rise to meet it. As a result, you will have respect from other people that you did not have before.

—Your relationships will improve. Whether you are a mom, wife, girlfriend, sister, friend, boss or employee, your relationships will become different.

Those that were already good will get better; and in those relationships that are strained, you will find the courage and strength to improve them OR remove yourself from them. Being in relationships with people that contribute to your well-being is a huge benefit!

—You will see pretty quickly when people engage with you only to mistreat, use or abuse you. When you matter, you see that you deserve to be in relationships that lift you up, not hold you down. You will find the courage to stand up for yourself and what is important to you.

—You will make decisions confidently. You will trust that you are competent and will not be paralyzed by indecision. You will no longer defer to the opinions of others, spin wildly or flip flop.

—You will find your voice. You will be able to express your opinions much easier. Conflict will not be something that you shy away from. You will no longer be worried about exposing yourself, so you can be unapologetically real and honor the voice inside.

—Your energy levels will skyrocket. When you are no longer waging the internal battles of self-doubt, fear and second guessing everything you do, you will find the "tired feeling" goes away. You will have plenty of energy to enjoy life!

—Your health will improve. Continued levels of stress are not good for your body. The stress that your body goes through when you are wearing your game face is tremendous. You will have energy to take care of yourself. You will sleep better. You will stress less and you will find yourself wanting to eat better and exercise more because you won't want to go backwards. You will want the best for yourself because you know you are worth it.

—You will be more productive. That's right – all of the energy that you used for waging the internal struggles or fighting against the negativity around you, can now be used for better things. You will find you can accomplish tasks in a much shorter time and you will become more creative. When your mind is free to create positive things instead of fighting or hiding the negative, you will be amazed at what can happen.

—You will get more out of life. When you are free to have fun and experiment and enjoy the freedom that choices can bring you, life becomes much better. When you climb out of being stuck, you will find that you enjoy interacting with people. You will want to do more than just sit at home or tend to the daily chores of life. You will want to get out and LIVE!

—You will feel peace. There is tremendous peace and contentment when you embrace confidence at your core. When you get a taste of how good it can be, you will do everything you can to protect that peace and remove what threatens it.

—Negativity won't stay for long. That peace you discover is more powerful than anything else you will
experience. When negative conversations with
yourself begin and you start to doubt who you are or
if you are worthy, it doesn't last long. You might
have a bad day or two, but they are the exception
rather than the rule.

—Your loneliness disappears. Wearing the game
face can be a lonely place. Once you remove it, and
truly own your value, you don't feel lonely anymore.
When you are content in who you are, you are okay
with spending time alone because you do not need
validation from other people. You will not feel compelled to seek approval from others or to perform to
receive affirmation from those around you.

The sole prize is not merely achieving confidence.
Confidence is actually the vehicle to achieve the
benefits I just outlined. The true prize is what you
are able to achieve because you feel confidence at
the core level. The energy you send off as a result
of feeling confidence at your core is much different
than without it. All of it compounds to propel you
to achieve bigger results than you thought were pos-
sible.

By the time you complete all of the key activities,
you will have a solid foundation of who you are and
what is important to you. You will learn how to
communicate better, how to draw boundaries better, how to create an environment that inspires your
success and how to reframe your choices. You will
no longer wade in that sea of mediocrity. There is so

much on the line, but the rewards on the other side are phenomenal!

One piece of advice: Write it down!

You will want to keep a record of your activities and what you have discovered. You can use what you have written as a guide if you are ever tempted to wear the game face again and choose to deny your value.

There may be times when life knocks you down, but rather than resort to self-doubt and fear, you can reread what you recorded and be reminded of what you are worth. You will see how much you have already overcome and how much farther ahead you are because of the combination of experiences you have had.

What will the benefits be in YOUR life for discovering Confidence at your Core?

—Chapter Nine—
The First Key =
<u>P</u>ersonal Inventory

It is necessary to take stock of who you are and what is important to you. Self-inspection can be hard. You may not always like what you see. If you don't complete this round of activities, the rest won't matter. This is the reason we are here. You get to discover who you are and what you are made of.

When you complete each of the activities, please be sure to choose a celebration. You will continue with what feels good. Reward yourself — some of this is exhausting work.

The following are some areas that deserve your attention. The more examples you can come up with the better. Really dig deep and don't let yourself off the hook with only a few answers for each activity.

DO YOURSELF A FAVOR AND DO THE WORK!!

Activity One: *What parts of your body do you appreciate? Your body is your temple and surely you can find at least some functions that you are grateful for! If you need to find inspiration, look in the mirror and really notice just how beautiful you are!*

You may suffer from poor body image or just take for granted the amazing creation your body can be. Remembering some of your better features is a good way to call to mind how valuable you are.

Activity Two: *What character traits do you value most about yourself and how do you use them?*

When your focus becomes negative, it is easy to forget that you possess valuable traits and that you actually do things well. You weren't created to be useless or horrible at everything. Taking some time to remember what you are good at is vital to reframing your confidence level.

Activity Three: *Take ten minutes or longer to go outside and observe nature today. It may seem to be too hot or too cold, but it is only ten minutes — you can do it! Observe what you see, feel, smell, and hear. Everything that you encounter is a gift created for you just because you are loved. Write down your observations and how it makes you feel to be so loved.*

The beauty found in nature was created for you to enjoy! If you can take a few moments to recognize how beautiful something may be and to remember that it was created merely for your pleasure – what a boost to your ego!

Activity Four: *What five people do you admire or are inspired by? They do not necessarily need to be people who you know, but can be people who you are exposed to in some way. It is important to also identify why you feel that way. Is it a quality they possess? Something they do for you? An example that they set?*

Recognize the goodness and value that other people bring to your life. If you admire a particular quality in someone else, it means that you are capable of recognizing value in people. You gain confidence when you have positive people to influence you.

You may want to take it a step further and actually reach out to the people on your list. It is easy to distance yourself from others when you aren't feeling your best. It is also a great burst of inspiration to be in contact with people who make you feel good. Think about how you would feel if someone reached out to you and told you they were inspired by you. Extend that same courtesy. The rewards will be abundant.

Activity Five: *When was the last time you did something for yourself? How did you "treat" yourself? Did you get a massage? Take a bath? Exercise? Read a book? How long has that been? Take a few minutes right now and plan one activity each week for the next month that takes care of you. Put it on your calendar and make sure you do it!*

Self-care can be one of the most powerful things you do. There is a reason the airlines tell you to place your oxygen mask on first before assisting others. It is essential to take care of the gift you are!

Activity Six: *How do you enjoy spending time? Take a few minutes to connect with what you would enjoy doing if you could spend your time in any way. Think back to what you enjoyed as a child. Think about what you would do if you had no time or money constraints. Identify activities that make your soul happy.*

This is important!! Making these types of activities a part of your daily life increases the confidence you feel.

Activity Seven: *Recall at least a few situations when you were pleased with the outcome. Identify what you did that made a difference to the outcome. Write down what satisfied you about your part in the situation. Enjoy the smile of satisfaction knowing you did a good job!*

When you are feeling less-than-confident, it is easy to think that you don't handle anything well. You may feel that you allow other people to have power and that the relationship or situation is never balanced. Tap into a few times when there was a balance. Remember that if you did it once, you can do it again. This activity will change your perspective — you CAN achieve a more confident stance.

Activity Eight: *How would you enjoy making money? If you could make money in any way, what would you choose to do? Do not concern yourself with HOW it could happen, just identify what you would want to do if you could do anything that you were passionate about.*

Performing a job you are passionate about increases your desire to participate and achieve success. Being stuck in a job or money-making venture that does not fulfill you leaves you feeling less than confident. Explore the options and feel the shift in your energy and focus.

Activity Nine: *What could you do to be a blessing to people? How would you do it? Who would you bless? How would you feel when you bless someone? The activity is to imagine what you would do, but you get BIG bonus points if you actually carry out one or more of these blessings.*

When you reach out and touch other people's lives to help them, you build confidence from doing something positive for others. If you are concentrating on someone else's life, it takes the focus off of the difficulties in your own.

Activity Ten: *What are some weaknesses you may possess? When you examine what you perceive as a weakness, think of a situation where it could actually become a strength. Try reframing* *that weakness into a positive quality rather than a negative one.*

Sometimes you are fooled into believing that you are only made up of areas in which you do not excel. In fact, there are situations when those qualities can be an asset. You were given everything you need to have a life of hope and a future—how can even the weaknesses help you?

Activity Eleven: *Identify how you would like to be remembered.*

Legacy is huge. You get to choose how people remember you! If your actions and interactions are not making the impact you want them to, you have the POWER to change that.

Activity Twelve: *What were some lessons you learned from a negative situation? How did it make you feel about yourself and your abilities? Do you recognize that even something perceived as negative can turn into a positive with the right mindset?*

Learning is at the heart of our personal power. If you are learning, you are gaining confidence.

Activity Thirteen: *List 50 things or people who you are grateful for.   Fifty may seem like more than you can handle; but once you get started, you will see it won't be too difficult.*

Gratitude can be a huge game changer! You can't be negative and truly grateful! Remember, the things and people you are grateful for were placed in your life for a reason — to help you learn, grow or feel loved. That is pretty powerful all by itself!

Activity Fourteen: *How do you honor and respect yourself? Do you speak to yourself or about yourself in a way that demonstrates respect? Identify how you show those ideals in your conversations and by your actions. If you can't think of ways that you are presently honoring yourself, come up with ways that you will begin to take care of who you are.*

The most abusive relationship most of us will ever have is with ourselves. If you aren't respecting who you are, why would anyone else? When your actions and language demonstrate respect, others will follow your lead.

Activity Fifteen: *What inspires you? Think of a quote, Scripture or even a single word that inspires you. Whatever you choose should be something you would get a boost from seeing every day — something that would encourage you to keep going* *even when you feel like giving up.*

Connecting with what touches your soul is a great way to build confidence. When you identify what that inspiration is, display it where you can see it daily. You can use it as a reminder to check if the decisions you are making are in line with your goals set up by your inspiration statement.

Activity Sixteen: *What would your "ideal" reality look like? Who would be in your life? What would you spend your time doing? How would you feel? Next think about what your "current" reality looks and feels like. Is there a disconnect? Identify the areas that are not connected.*

Sometimes you have to create a picture in your mind of who you want to be. Then you can create a plan to make that vision a reality. Uncover the vision first and the actions to achieve it will be easier to recognize. Your ability to plan will improve your confidence.

Now it is time to recognize your value. This can be a tough one. If you own your value, then it means you possess traits that you deem valuable. The personal inventory you just took is a great way to hit the highlights.

You identified situations you handled well, your passions, what makes you happy, what fulfills you, who and what you appreciate and more. Let's connect the dots on your personal inventory.

Activity Seventeen: *What three things did you learn about yourself in the previous activities that surprised you in a positive way?*

Activity Eighteen: *What are the top five attributes that you value in yourself and why they are important to you?*

Activity Nineteen: *Now list why you deserve to take care of yourself. What will be the benefits to you and those around you? Provide at least three reasons.*

Activity Twenty: *Why do you deserve to have good things happen to you? ("I don't" is not the answer you are aiming for either.)*

It can be hard to reframe your thinking in a positive slant. Stop denying your value and realize the reasons you have to be confident that have been there all of the time. Now that you have had the opportunity to identify why you are worthy, that you possess many positive traits and talents, and that you have been blessed with life and the opportunity to succeed and grow, you can embrace the value of who you are.

—The First Key = Personal Inventory, 9

Your Thoughts

You Had It All Along —

Your Thoughts

—The First Key = Personal Inventory, 9

Your Thoughts

You Had It All Along —

Your Thoughts

—The First Key = Personal Inventory, 9

Your Thoughts

—Chapter Ten—
The Second Key =
<u>O</u>pen Communication

How you communicate your value to others plays a vital role in your confidence. Chances are you may be communicating that you really do not possess the value you want people to believe you do. I realized I was saying many things that were expressing exactly how I felt about myself and it wasn't a positive picture.

There are a few key phrases you may say that are strong indicators that you truly aren't as confident as you would like others to believe.

The first one is "I'm sorry." Now, of course, that is a phrase that should be used in appropriate situations when you have genuinely done something that deserves an apology. That is not what I am talking about. This is an excessive use of the phrase. You apologize for things that have absolutely nothing to do with you and are not anywhere near your realm of control. All of the blanket apologies you make are really indicators that you are sorry that you aren't valuable. On a subconscious level, you may believe that you are responsible for the trials in this life because you do not possess enough worth.

One day I made a note of all the times I said that I was sorry. I was shocked at how many times in just one day that I uttered those words. Most times weren't for anything I could even do anything about. I felt a responsibility that I shouldn't have. When I stopped saying it in excessive levels, my perspective began to shift about who I was.

Have you ever uttered the phrase "You can mess with me, but not my _____!" You can fill in the blank with whatever you feel passionate about – your kids, your friends, your pets, your success. Let the weight of that statement sink in for a minute.

You can mess with me.

You are giving people permission to treat you badly. Maybe you don't feel like you are worthy of anything different. You must ask yourself if that is the message you want to be sending?

The last phrase that is a real tell-tale sign of your confidence level is "I can't." You declare that you can't do something or be with someone because hidden on a subconscious level you don't feel like you deserve it. You pass on opportunities because you aren't sure you can succeed. You avoid conflict because you believe you can't handle the outcome. You deny your opinions and emotions because you either can't imagine anyone else caring, or that your opinion might make a difference. "I can't" is a spirit killer and you probably say it more than you should.

Communication begins within. You must start by changing the conversation that goes on inside your head. Every day you most likely speak to yourself in harsh language and it becomes a habit. You may not even realize that you are doing it. The negative conversation must be changed to a positive one if you are going to see any different results.

How you are communicating your worth to your-self? Do not pass judgment, just acknowledge what it is. If the way you are communicating with your-self does not serve you well, then take steps to change it.

Next observe how you are communicating your val-ue with others. Are you using negative vocabulary? Do you demean yourself? Do you take blame for things beyond your control? Do you succumb to others' influences and rarely assert your own opin-ions/desires? Honest answers to all of these ques-tions will give you a better picture of how you are communicating your worth to the world.

Finding your voice is crucial after uncovering your value. You just took a really good look at yourself and probably realized that you have gifts and talents well beyond what you gave yourself credit for. It isn't enough to discover them, please share them. There is no one like you and the world deserves to know you, not just the mask you hide behind.

Using your voice takes practice, but it makes a real difference. Using language that builds you up ra-ther than tears you down is important. Asserting how you really feel and being unafraid to speak, de-spite the idea that some people are not going to agree, should not negate your value. Their disap-proval clearly is a statement about them, not you. When you can grasp that, the process gets even eas-ier.

Begin with practicing "I statements." State how you feel and you may even want to throw in why. At first, you don't even have to say your "I statements" out loud. Get comfortable with creating the thoughts first until it becomes more natural for you to acknowledge how you feel.

Eventually attempt to use your voice. Maybe you can start with the mirror and as that becomes more comfortable, try it out on people. Eventually, it will become second nature to assert how you feel and to communicate your value with ease.

What areas of your life would improved communication be a benefit?

If you could express one thought to the world, what would it be?

—Chapter Eleven—
The Third Key =
<u>W</u>ell-Drawn Boundaries

Drawing boundaries can be tough, but when you manage it, it will make the most difference. So many times you can get held hostage by the negativity of others and world events. It is easy to let that negativity dictate and raise questions of your worth.

You could be the most amazing person on earth but if you do not expect and require other people to treat you that way, then you will have gained little. By not requiring a higher level of respect from others, then you are really sending a message that you do not value who you are. Drawing boundaries is crucial to your success.

Begin by answering these questions to see if you need to place stronger boundaries in your life.

—Do you tolerate name calling? Being made fun of? Blanket insults?

—Do you tolerate negative comments and attitudes from others?

—Do you automatically defer to the opinions of others rather than asserting your own?

—Do you allow others to violate your personal space?

—Do you voice your concerns or make your opinions known? Do you squelch your feelings and expectations out of fear of what others will think?

—Do you agree to participate in activities or behaviors even though you do not want to?

—Do you allow other people to waste your time and energy? Do you share how it affects you when they do that?

—Do you silently suffer so as to not rock the boat or upset other people?

All of these are indications that you are placing the value of others on a greater level than you place your own.

It is time to stand up for who you are!

When you treat yourself with respect then others will rise to meet it. If they do not, then the question becomes if that person is really the best influence to have in your life.

Please do not be afraid to weed out the negativity that may have gotten you into this situation in the first place. No matter what, you deserve respect.

Place boundaries to protect who you are and your value.

List how and where you can draw boundaries in your life. Be fearless in protecting your value!

This key is usually easier said than done. My advice is to begin by defining your boundaries and then use those "I statements" you practiced in the last key. People tend to respond better if you aren't accusing them of disrespecting you.

There will be some push back when you start enforcing your boundaries. Expect it and be prepared to determine if those people actually belong in your life. I am not advocating that you dismiss all disrespectful people, but that is definitely a choice you can make.

If you have made it this far, you have completed some really good work! I hope that you are celebrating today. You are well on your way to confidence at your core!

Your Thoughts

—Chapter Twelve—
The Fourth Key =
<u>E</u>nvironment

There are two types of environments - the internal and the external. The work you have completed so far has really helped you "clean up and organize" your internal environment. As a former home stager and re-designer, I would be remiss in saying that your physical environment doesn't play a crucial part of your internal one. They both need to be in synch for effective change to take place.

First envision yourself in the place that you spend the most time. What does it look like? If you were to walk into that space, how would it make you feel? (This exercise will work in your personal and professional spaces.)

Next think about the emotions you want your space to evoke in you.

Observe the two sets of emotions – the ones you have and the ones you want. Is there a disconnect between the two? If there is, what are two immediate things could you do to remedy that?

Redesigning a space to reflect the personality and emotional needs of the user can be a daunting task and I am not recommending that you know how to do that or where to begin. The key here is to start recognizing how your environment contributes to your well-being.

If your space evokes stress because of clutter or disorganization, then it is not serving you well.

If the space where you need to be productive is dull, drab and lifeless, you may have a difficult time being effective in it. If your space is decorated around the needs and desires of someone else, there will be hidden resentments that may keep you from realizing true peace.

There is plenty of psychology and skills involved in the placement of furnishings, color and texture choices, but that is not what this step is all about.

This is designed to help you see where the disconnect may be and to be thinking about ways for you to replace the elements of your environment that do not serve you well with ones that do. Please understand the importance of being surrounded by a space that inspires you and reflects your value.

Here are a couple of practical tips on how to begin moving towards a more inspiring space.

—Identify and remove the items in the room that hold negative energy. Maybe you have a photo of you and your co-workers at a company function. You love the people, but got laid off your job and are harboring feelings of resentment. Each time you see that photo, you think about how unfair it was that you were let go, and your resentment builds. Take a new photo with your friends to inspire a more positive way of thinking.

—You may tend to hold onto things much longer than you need to. Usually this is caused by guilt.

It is fine to let go of items that do not serve you well. It doesn't mean you must remove them completely, just out of everyday view.

—Surround yourself with items and colors that inspire you. Maybe you put up art work that helps you instantly recall a vacation or stress-free kind of mood when you see it. Go ahead and make a vision board to keep your goals and dreams front and center. Put up photos of people, places or events that are important to you.

What are YOUR costs to not living or working in an inspiring space?

How could you benefit if you did create a more inspiring space?

—Chapter Thirteen—
The Fifth Key =
<u>R</u>eframing Your Choices

It is this step that helped me truly realize that I held the power when it came to developing confidence at my core. You possess the same power. And YES! You have had it all along.

Please realize that you have the power to choose what happens. You were loved enough to be given the power of choice. You may not always be able to choose yourself out of a situation, but you can always choose your reaction to it. No one can do that but you.

There is a great deal of responsibility in that statement because it removes assigning blame to others. It can be a hard pill to swallow to know that you are responsible. So you tend to say, "No, thank you" to new opportunities, because if it doesn't work out you get to accept responsibility. Playing the victim card can be much easier than deciding to change your circumstances.

When you are feeling lost and broken, it is easy to blame other people for your circumstances. You feel "this" way because "that" happened. There is also the notion that "I will feel better when/if this happens." You are giving your power away to other people or situations. Claim that power for who it was intended for – YOU!

Yes, you get to make the decision: *Is the game face going to define me or can I rise above and achieve more?* There are so many times when you fall into a survivalist mentality and do only what you need to do to get through each day. I understand sometimes that is all you are capable of, but there will be a defining moment when you get to reclaim that power. Reframing your choices takes practice and can be difficult, but is absolutely worth it. When you see the evidence that you can do it — you will feel empowered. You will finally achieve confidence at your core!

There is a multitude of negativity in the world today. These forces are at work in your life at every twist and turn. You have the power to choose a more positive way. Remember, it is *your* choice if negative events or behaviors define you. If you want to see the good in the world and you want to respect the value you possess, you hold that power. No one can take it from you without your permission.

DO NOT GRANT PERMISSION!!

What are three situations or relationships in your life where you can use this powerful way of thinking to change the dynamics? What would happen? How would you benefit from choosing to honor your value more than someone else's? What does that look like? How does it feel?

The idea of creating something more than what you have now can leave you feeling overwhelmed. That is okay. That is why you were asked to keep a record of what you discovered throughout the book. You can come back and visit it as often as you need to. Start with small steps and celebrate along the way. You will find that you will be closer to that ideal reality – without wearing the game face AND feeling confidence at your core — in no time.

—Chapter Fourteen—
The Challenge

Who you were when you began this process is not who you are in the end. You have changed and that is good. That was truly the goal. You were not satisfied with the way you were — whether that was because you were hiding behind your game face or had reached a barrier in your earnings or weren't fulfilled in your relationships. You picked up this book to change something and you have succeeded.

The challenge is to maintain those changes so you can emerge as who you ultimately want to become. Know that it is a process.

You are in the process of becoming.

The desire for something better was planted within you because you were destined for more than what you had. Surviving is not the only thing you are capable of. You have everything you need to thrive.

You have been given the keys to unlock the treasure of confidence at your core. It is not enough to just receive the information. Now is the time:

—To make the choice every day to honor who you are and communicate it in a way that commands respect.

—To draw your boundaries without apology. That may mean removing people or things out of your life because they do not serve you well.

—To create an environment in line with your intention. If you want to succeed, surround yourself with what inspires your success.

—To continue to choose for your highest good. Settling for the status quo because it is safer than venturing into the unknown should not be acceptable any longer.

Now you know the difference.

Knowing is not going to be enough. Accept the daily challenge to be a little better than you were the day before and create a plan to make it happen.

Confidence is a constant battle. The world wants to tear away the blanket of confidence you entered this world in, but that can only happen if you let it.

When you win the battle and claim your confidence, you will find that the world may succeed in knocking you down, but it will not be able to knock you out. With unshakable faith, you can rely on your ability to stand back up, say thank you for the lesson and continue on your journey.

You may have been searching for an answer or a sign for who to be or what to do. Be confident that you already have the answer you seek.

The beauty is that you had it all along.

----About the Author----

Sheila Kennedy seemed to have it all, until she found herself the divorced mother of a teenager daughter struggling to make a living. Armed with strong faith and confidence at her core, she built a new life for herself. She credits the removal of her mask of false confidence as the catalyst for success in her coaching practice, the J29Project.

Sheila began the J29 Project (www.j29project.com) to inspire and coach women with the skills and strategies she used to develop confidence at her core. Her signature P.O.W.E.R. Process is the foundation for helping women to live the life they deserve.

Confidence Coach, Speaker and Co-author of the Best Selling book, *Wounded? Survive! Thrive!!! 101 Women's Journeys from Torment to Triumph,* Sheila is an advocate for women achieving an unshakable faith in themselves and all of the amazing opportunities that confidence can bring.